P9-DTC-072

# THE WELL and THE CATHEDRAL

## BOOKS BY IRA PROGOFF

*At a Journal Workshop: The Basic Text and Guide
for Using the Intensive Journal*

*The Symbolic and the Real*

*Depth Psychology and Modern Man*

*The Death and Rebirth of Psychology*

*The Cloud of Unknowing*

*The Image of an Oracle*

*Jung's Psychology and Its Social Meaning*

*Jung, Synchronicity and Human Destiny*

*The Star/Cross*

*The White Robed Monk*

# THE WELL and THE CATHEDRAL

**With an Introduction on its Use
in the Practice of Meditation**

# Ira Progoff

Second edition enlarged

DIALOGUE HOUSE LIBRARY / NEW YORK

Published by Dialogue House Library
80 East 11 Street, New York, New York 10003
Copyright © 1972, 1977 by Ira Progoff
First Printing, 1971
Second Printing, 1972
Second Enlarged Edition, 1977
All rights reserved. Except for brief excerpts
quoted in reviews, no part of this publication may be reproduced, stored in a re-
trieval system or transmitted by any form
or by any means, electronic, mechanical,
photocopying, recording or otherwise without written permission of the publisher.

*Library of Congress Cataloging in Publication Data*

1. Meditations.   I   *The Well and the Cathedral*
BV4832.2P75        1976        2481.3        76-20823
ISBN 87941-004-3        Paperback ISBN 8794-005-01

Printed in the United States of America

*Dedicated to*

MATT ROBERTS

1925–1976

*Designer of the Intensive Journal Logo,*
*he had almost completed designing*
*this book when he was called away.*

*A friend beyond guile.*

# Table of Contents

*Part One*

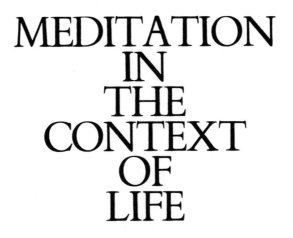

# MEDITATION
# IN
# THE
# CONTEXT
# OF
# LIFE

# 1. Introduction to the Second Edition

Twenty years ago I recommended taking a spiritual journey using a medieval text, *The Cloud of Unknowing*,[1] as a guide. Now I am suggesting a different kind of text, carrying a contemporary method of meditation but with the same purpose and a parallel thrust. Its purpose is to draw us into direct contact with the great unity of Being. Its thrust is to focus the energies of that contact into the creativity of our lives.

*The Well and the Cathedral* has emerged over a period of several years out of my personal practice with the disciplines of Process Meditation in conjunction with the *Intensive Journal*.[2] This text contains the heart of the Process Meditation approach and is a way of entry leading into the larger program.[3] Since it was published in its first experimental edition in 1971, *The Well and the Cathedral* has been tested and refined through its use in numerous contexts both religious and secular, in personal growth workshops, in meditation services and spiritual retreats.

The method of meditation in *The Well and the Cathedral* is carried by a sequence of eight cycles of experience. They neither describe the method, nor do they explain it. Instead they take you directly into the practice of meditation so you can know it by experiencing it; and you experience it by participating in it.

At this point I shall not attempt to explain its principles nor teach its methods. However you can learn to use these meditations yourself in the same way that a fish learns to swim: by finding itself in the water and doing what comes naturally. Later, in the sections that follow the text, we shall discuss the work in historical perspective, considering some of the concepts that underlie it and the ways of practicing it. But it is best to study and reflect upon the principles of this method of meditation only after we have worked with the text and have experienced its process at least once and perhaps several times. Our intellectual considerations and judgments can then be based on the facts of our inner experience.

One way to think of *The Well and the Cathedral* is as an *entrance meditation*. It is a means of entering the depths of our inner life. There are many theories about this inner realm, what it is and what it contains. Many philosophies speak of its mysteries, claim to describe it, and some even provide a roadmap telling what they believe can be found there.

But *The Well and the Cathedral* opens an additional possibility. It provides a means of actually entering inner space and finding out for ourselves what is there. It does not predetermine what we shall discover, how we shall experience it, nor how we shall describe what we find there and what we shall believe about it. Rather, *The Well and the Cathedral* takes us to the place of inner experience and allows us each to decide for ourselves.

Most important, *The Well and the Cathedral* is not a teaching of any particular view of truth, not a philosophy, a theory, nor a theological doctrine. As they take place one by one, the experiences that occur in this work cumulatively mark off a path that leads to contact with our inner levels. And yet the guidelines for this path are completely open-ended. They take us to a deep place and then leave us free, each to reach a larger dimension of reality within our own life context, in our own terms and at our own tempo.

Once we have entered our inner depths and have learned how to move about there as in a dimension of space, we are able to determine by our own authority which beliefs and philosophies are the most persuasive to us. At that point, however, when we are making our choices with respect to truth after working with *The Well and the Cathedral*, our decisions will not be based on intellectual ideas nor on the reports of experiences about which other persons have told us. Our spiritual conclusions can then be based on the direct knowing supplied by our own first hand experiences.

Primarily, *The Well and the Cathedral* is a meditative text that assists the process of personal centering by providing a way inward. In addition, it is a text that carries with it a method of meditation not limited to particular doctrines. In this sense it is an ecumenical means of deepening spiritual experience. It provides a way of personal practice and inner discipline that enables an individual to reach progressively deeper levels in meditation.

Since this method of meditation is flexible and open-ended, it can be used either by itself or in conjunction with other programs. It may be used alone in an individual's privacy or in a group setting. It tends to complement and support other psychological approaches and other styles of religious practice. In my observation, it does not conflict with them.

The structure of *The Well and the Cathedral* is a sequence of meditations that move inward by degrees, each unit carrying us a step further, opening another dimension of experience, and generating another measure of spiritual energy. The text was originally published in 1971 on an exploratory basis. Since then, in the course of two printings, it has been used experimentally in numerous religious and non-religious contexts.

These explorations have repeatedly indicated that *The Well and the Cathedral* is especially helpful in those situations where a deepening in the level of experience is required. This has been the case in both secular and spiritual areas, and particularly where the two overlap. It establishes an atmosphere for prayer, and it is helpful in psychotherapy.

Sections of *The Well and the Cathedral* have been used in numerous religious situations to set the base for experiential services not limited by doctrine. It seems to have a particular value in stimulating spontaneous inner experience in individuals while maintaining the tone of prayer and devotion. In this sense, the experiences to which *The Well and the Cathedral* leads involve a new kind of religious freedom. More than a freedom to believe in the religious doctrines of one's choice, it is a religious freedom to reach out and experiment in total openness on the dimension of spiritual reality. In this respect, an increasing number of priests and sisters are using *The Well and the Cathedral* when conducting spiritual retreats, combining it with the Intensive Journal Process.

As this edition goes to press, I have been particularly interested to learn how *The Well and the Cathedral* is being used in college philosophy courses. The principle being followed there has broad implications for the relation of the intellect to spiritual experience. It suggests that intellectual analysis can be carried out most fruitfully when it is done within an atmosphere of deep inner experience. First the inner experience, then the thinking and philosophizing about it, followed by further and still deeper experiences.

In this regard, a specific hypothesis on the relation of meditation to education is that, when students have had inner experiences, they are in a better position to understand what the great figures, Plato and Aristotle, Spinoza and Leibnitz and Whitehead have been talking about. Then they can have equivalent awarenesses of their own. Strengthening this possibility, one of the units of meditation in *The Well and the Cathedral* (Section VII) sets the base for and leads directly into an exercise that enables students to establish a direct dialogue relationship with those persons who are sources of wisdom in our culture.

An additional unanticipated use of *The Well and the Cathedral* lies in its relation to Eastern ways of meditation. While the two approaches are quite separate, of course, many persons have reported that when their outer life was so jangled that they could not reach an inner contact by their accustomed practices, *The Well and the Cathedral* quieted their inner atmosphere and enabled them to proceed with their regular spiritual disciplines.

Similar experiences have been reported by persons preparing for particular ritual observances, or prayer and contemplation within a more explicitly Western religious context. *The Well and the Cathedral* lends support and prepares the way. In this sense it truly serves as an *entrance* to meditation, opening a path inward whether to enter Oriental meditation, Christian prayer and contemplation or Hebraic worship.

As an Entrance Meditation, *The Well and the Cathedral* opens a doorway into a large house of spiritual experience and it lets each of us choose our own room.

## References

1. *The Cloud of Unknowing*, a Modern Rendering with an Introductory Commentary by Ira Progoff, Delta Paperback, New York, 1957.
2. Ira Progoff, *At a Journal Workshop*, The Basic Text and Guide for using the Intensive Journal, Dialogue House Library, New York, 1975.
3. Ira Progoff, *Process Meditation*, scheduled for publication by Dialogue House Library during 1977.

# 2. The Cycles of Meditation

Some of us will prefer to do this meditative work alone in our own privacy. Some will prefer to do it in the company of others. Many of us will very likely conclude that a combination of the two is most fruitful. Each of us, to fit our own rhythm, can personally work out a balanced combination of meditation practice in religious services, in workshops, in classes, and especially in the solitude that carries the continuity of our inner disciplines and garners the cumulative results.

In whatever circumstances we use *The Well and the Cathedral*, it is always a work of privacy. This is inherent in its method. We keep our attention focused on our inward movement. While we are engaged in the work, we do not let ourselves be diverted into conversation. We do not discuss and examine with others what is taking place inside us, lest we thereby break into its inward momentum and interrupt its process.

Especially, we do not compare our experiences with anyone because to do so would cause us to become judgmental of ourselves and of others. Such comparisons also cause us to become self-conscious while we are engaged in our inner work. But most important, comparing our inner experiences and talking about them with other persons has the effect of turning our attention outward so that we are looking at our inner life from the outside thereby separating us from our inner process. Being at one with our inner process is the essence of the work of meditation.

Whatever breaks the unity of the inner connection is to be avoided in this work. Remain within the flow of it so as to build its continuity and momentum in every way you can. Remember that the process works best when we do not think *about* our meditation but when we *are* our meditation. If our meditation is *about* something, we will not be able to prevent it from becoming a form of thought rather than a direct experience; and in that case our meditation will be drawn up toward the cerebral levels at the surface of our being.

Throughout this work we should bear in mind that meditation is an inward activity with no object other than encouraging the spiritual process of *being and becoming* within the person. Subject and object are thus not separate in the act of meditation, but are one. The unfolding of our inner being is a unitary process without divisions. The key to our inward work, therefore, lies in our *being our meditation* rather than self-consciously thinking about it. For this reason we remain totally within our experience once the process begins. We do not step outside of our meditation to be aware of what is happening, to comment on it, think about it, talk about it, or compare our experiences with others. We are so much *in* it that we *are* it. We *are* it, especially as it continues its inner movement and as it builds its momentum in the depth of us.

In using *The Well and the Cathedral*, the carriers of the progressive experience are the eight cycles of meditation that comprise the text. Each of these establishes an atmosphere at a particular level and draws us into the depths of the Self by means of a philosophically neutral set of symbols. Entering the process by means of these symbols, we soon find we are moving on a track of inner experience that is not shaped by the symbols but is altogether our own. We are, in fact, using the units of meditation as vehicles for our own deepening explorations.

As we work with them, each of the units of meditation becomes a cycle of experience in a special sense. It begins by taking us into a quiet place, then enlarging the span of our consciousness and activating the flow of imagery that is not only visual but uses all our means of perception, outer and inner. As these experiences are stirred in us, they generate their own energies, building a movement that carries us over a broad range of inner terrain before coming to rest. The pause that follows this activity gives us an opportunity to record what has taken place and to let the many implications seep into the deep corners of our being.

In working with these cycles of meditative experience, our first step is to read a unit to ourselves, or hear it read at a meditation workshop or service, or to play it on a cassette. We let it draw us into stillness, then we move with it. We do not think about it nor evaluate it nor interpret it. We simply enter the meditation, become part of it and go with it without seeking to direct the inner phenomena in any way. We let them happen without benefit of our guidance, since we trust the principle of life-integration that moves through the inner process.* We do not seek to "assist" it with our minds, lest we thereby intrude and spoil it. But we do observe what takes place from the vantage point of a neutral, albeit very interested, bystander.

Presently it becomes necessary for us to begin recording our experiences. We allow enough time for the free inner movement to proceed, but not too much. We should not let the inner process move so far by itself that we accumulate more perceptions then we can remember, lest we forget them before

* For a description of the principles of self-balancing and life-integration as they operate in the transitions of a human life, see Progoff, *At a Journal Workshop*, Ch. XX, p. 290 ff.

21

we can write them down. On the other hand, we do not wish to disrupt the flow of our experiences and thus break our inner momentum. The key lies in maintaining a balance, a rhythm between the inner perception and the outer recording. It is a rhythm to which we become attuned after a little practice.

The best way to proceed seems to be to learn to go back and forth from the inner to the outer levels, and back inward again. In time we become accustomed to making quick, brief but adequate, entries. Writing them from the deep place with our eyes only slightly open, these entries will often be barely legible when we seek to read them. If, however, we return to rewrite them without letting too long a period elapse, the inner events will be fresh enough in our minds so that we can transcribe and enlarge them, even with only a few barely legible words to guide us. Afterwards we should take as much time as we need to describe in detail all that has taken place, amplifying the nuances and elaborating any points that may be significant to us when we read them back to ourselves weeks or even months in the future.

The *Meditation Log* on the left hand page of this edition is intended to give you an easily accessible place to make your brief descriptions while stlll in the deep atmosphere of your meditation. Later, when you fill in the details of your entries, you can transcribe them onto other sheets, incorporating them into your Intensive Journal or whatever other system you use for maintaining the record of your inner life.

Those of us who have already had the experience of working with the Intensive Journal, either by participating in an actual Journal Workshop or by following the exercises described in *At A Journal Workshop* will know how to feed the entries made in the *Meditation Log* into the other sections of the Journal by practicing the *Journal Feedback* exercises. By means of that program, the experiences that are stimulated through the practice of meditation serve as a source of inner life material that contributes great energies and awareness to the larger process of continuing personal development.

For those of us who have not yet worked with the *Intensive Journal Process,* the *Meditation Log* will serve a similar, although preliminary, function. Use it to record and collect the spontaneous experiences and feelings that occur as you are working in the depth of yourself. As you enlarge on your first brief entries and as you transcribe them, they will grow in volume. You will undoubtedly then want to use a separate notebook to contain them whether you incorporate them into the Intensive Journal Process or not. If you continue working with them, enlarging them as you transcribe them into a separate notebook, reading them back to yourself at a later time, reentering the experiences in order to expand them, you will find that the entries originally collected in your *Meditation Log* become the base for a larger spiritual workbook and an ongoing personal program of meditation. It will naturally expand as you proceed with the work, and as you deepen your level of inner contact.

In this context we can see the close interrelationship between the use of the Intensive Journal and the work of meditation. They complement and support each other. The Intensive Journal provides a large canvas on which the movement of our whole personal history can lay itself out before us. Our work in meditation, especially as we move with the cycles of *The Well and the Cathedral,* draws us to depths of our Being where a greater-than-personal principle of self-balancing becomes effective within us. Water, it is said, finds its own level, and so does the movement of our individual existence when we practice meditation in the context of our life history. We gain access to a quality of wisdom and a capacity for inner guidance that gives direction and meaning to our lives.

As we move through our sequence of meditations, each unit takes us a little further inward. We proceed a step at a time. At the close of each meditation, we pause, enter into the silence, and let new experiences and awarenesses come to us. We remain in that silence for as long as feels right to us, and for as long as new perceptions, unguided and unsolicited, continue to come to us from within.

There is a simple rule to follow as to how long we remain in the silence. It is this: when you are just about ready to come back up and leave the silence, that is the time to go back inward, to wait in open stillness, and to let the process move a little deeper than before.

# 3. Entering the Work

Many of us will find as we are working with *The Well and the Cathedral* that while we are reading the text to ourselves we are inwardly hearing the words as though they were being spoken to us. Sometimes it will be helpful to hear them actually read aloud either by ourselves or by others, as at a meditation workshop or service, or by using the tape recording of the text.* The sound of the spoken word often makes an important contribution to the deepening of the atmosphere and thus helps us move inward.

With this in mind the following instructions, which are intended to lead us each into our individual experience with the cycles of meditation, are given in a form that is very similar to the Prologue on the cassette.

Since *The Well and the Cathedral* is a sequence of meditations, we move through them section by section, proceeding a step at a time until, at the close, or when we have worked with the entire cycle perhaps three or four times, the cumulative effect

---

* A cassette reading by Ira Progoff of the full text of *The Well and the Cathedral* accompanies this edition. It is available from Dialogue House Library.

and the meaning of the whole becomes clear to us.

It is good to read one section at a time and then to have a substantial period of silence. It is important that we allow sufficient time between units of meditation so that new experiences can come to us, and so that we can be free to move with them, explore their possibilities, and record them as fully as they require.

As we come to the close of each section, the phrase, "In the Silence . . . In the Silence," is repeated. That is the cue for each of us to enter our own silence. With the reading as our starting point, we let the meditative experience move freely within us, following its own rhythms and drawing forth its own contents. We allow it to proceed in its own way. As it moves on, we take note of whatever it gives us. We record whatever forms it takes, whether there are visions that we see, words that we hear, new thoughts and plans that come to us, intuitions or awarenesses, emotions, body sensations, experiences of unity with nature, with God, with the universe. Whatever they may be, we take note of them. We acknowledge them and we record them in our *Meditation Log*.

With the phrase, "In the Silence," we begin the period of stillness in which the meditation works actively within us. We let it have all the time it desires. More silence is better than too little. There must be time both for the silence itself and for recording what we have experienced. Then we move on to the next section.

It is important to bear in mind that we are not directing our meditations along any particular channel. We do not favor one path or symbolism over any other. As much as possible we let ourselves be altogether free and open so that an unrestricted range of unguided experiences may come to us at the interior level. We observe them all, accept them without judgment and without restriction, then record them and continue.

No particular type of experience is of itself better than any other. It will be helpful at all times if we can bear in mind that we are working in a *process* of meditation, and that the nature of a process is that it passes through many phases and changes. All the varied experiences and awarenesses that come to us are equally valid parts of this process. None is possible without the others. Therefore we accept them all and we record them without censoring or editing them.

We work in one unit of meditation at a time and then proceed to the next. The experiences we have in each unit will not be separate, however. We find that the imagery and ideas that come to us in one section recur in another, very often presenting themselves in a further phase of development. In each case, we accept it and record it just as it comes to us. We do not reject any inner experiences because they seem to be unimportant or because they do not interest us at the moment. We accept them and we record them just as we experience them. Later when we reread our descriptions of them, we shall find that they fall into place in the context of our moving process. Some may still seem unimportant to us, and we may bypass them at that time. Others will stimulate us further and we may extend them. They are all part of the continuity of the meditative process that builds and deepens within each of us in our own rhythm, in our own life context, and in our own timing.

To support this process we record all the experiences that come to us. We may use either the *Meditation Log* pages in this edition, or separate sheets that we shall later incorporate into our Intensive Journal. Many of us will choose to combine the two procedures, using the *Meditation Log* pages to record the spontaneous experiences that come to us with each reading, and at a later time transferring them to our permanent Journal. We should not neglect to record the date on which each entry is made, for the time and sequence of our experiences become an increasingly meaningful piece of information to us as we continue with our inner work. In addition, we shall very likely discover that the act of transferring our entries will become a valuable experience in itself, stimulating us to expand our original material. Thus it will take us still a step further in our inner process.

We regard our work of meditation as an ongoing process of progressive deepening. We continue it and we return to it again and again, working at it sometimes a little at a time, sometimes with great intensity and with great fervor.

We go with it as it goes with us. It proceeds by a self-guiding and self-balancing principle. Therefore we trust it as we are drawn to deeper levels within ourselves.

Now we become quiet, centering in stillness, and we give ourselves over to the inner process. We shall be ready to record our experiences as they come to us.

> Meanwhile we relax in silence,
> Letting the Self become still,
> Letting our breath become slow,
> Letting our thoughts come to rest.

*Part Two*

# THE
# WELL
# AND
# THE
# CATHEDRAL

# I

## *Muddy/Clear:*
## *The Mirror of the Water*

*Meditation Log*  *Date*

1.  I remember the saying
    Of the old wise man, Lao Tse:
        "Muddy water,
        Let stand
        Becomes clear."

2.  Thinking of that,
    I look within myself.
    I see,
    On the screen of my mind's eye,
    A stream of water,
    Moving,
    Swirling,
    Murky,
    It is full of things.
    I cannot look into this water.
    I cannot see my reflection
    In this water.

*Meditation Log*                    *Date*

3.     Now the movement stops.
The water is in one place.
It is heavy colored,
Muddy
But it is becoming quiet,
The water is at rest.
In its stillness
The muddiness
Is settling to the bottom.

4.     At the surface it becomes clear,
Transparent.
I can see into the water
More and more.
Now I can see through
To the very depth of it.
There it shines
And it reflects.

*Meditation Log*                    *Date*

5.   The heavens are reflected
     In the quiet water.
     It is clear.
     I see the reflection of a tree
     In the quiet water.
     The muddy water
     Has become clear.

6.   As I continue to look
     Into the stillness
     A reflection of myself
     Begins to appear.
     Deep in the quietness
     Of the water,
     I see
     A reflection of myself,
     Myself
     In many different forms.

*Meditation Log*                    *Date*

7.  I sit
    In the stillness
    And let the image shape itself.
    It becomes many things.
    Many images
    Appear in the still water,
    Many things
    Come up for me to see.

8.  In the depth of the water,
    The images
    That open the greatest vision
    Within me
    Are not those that are visible.
    I do not see them;
    I just know them.
    Something within me
    Recognizes them
    In the still water.

*Meditation Log*                    *Date*

9.  The muddy water has become quiet.
    I sit gazing into it,
    Seeing images,
    Visible and invisible,
    Letting them take form,
    Letting them change
    And re-form themselves
    In the depth of the still water,
    In the mirror of the water,
    In the depth of my Self,
    Moving, moving,
    In the Silence ... In the Silence.

*Meditation Log*                              *Date*

# II

## Feeling the Movement
## of Life

# Meditation Log

Date _____

1. We go further,
   Exploring the deep places,
   Exploring what is not known to us,
   Exploring the open possibilities
   Of our life.

2. We have become quiet.
   We have looked
   Into the stillness of the waters.
   Having entered that stillness,
   We have learned
   That emptiness refills itself.
   Emptiness refills itself
   To overflowing
   With new ideas,
   Awarenesses,
   Relationships,
   As life renews itself
   Out of itself.

*Meditation Log*                    *Date*

3.　Knowing that, we relax.
　　Emptiness refills itself.
　　We let go,
　　Breathing slowly,
　　Letting go,
　　Letting go of thoughts
　　As they move within us.
　　Each line of thought is free
　　To unfold in its own way.
　　Our thoughts being free,
　　We are free of them.
　　Our minds are quiet
　　As we are quiet.

4.　Our inner muscles,
　　The muscles of the spirit,
　　Are loose now,
　　Loose and limber,
　　Limber within ourselves,
　　Free and able to move
　　At the inward parts
　　Of our Self.

*Meditation Log*                    *Date*

5. We begin exploring
   In the stillness,
   Eyes closed,
   Feeling the movement of life,
   Our own life
   With its many phases,
   Cycles and changes,
   The changing movement of life,
   Our own life,
   The changing life of everyone.

6. Feeling the movement of life
   In all things
   And in everyone,
   Finding in the quiet water
   The elusive thread of life,
   Our life
   And the life of everyone,
   Retrieving the hidden thread
   Of meaning and direction
   In the movement of our life.

*Meditation Log*                                 *Date*

7. Exploring the deep places,
   Reaching inward
   To the memories and mysteries
   Of our life,
   Personal memories,
   And mysteries
   Much more than personal.

8. Restoring to ourselves
   The events of earlier years,
   Dreams fulfilled
   And unfulfilled,
   Plans and pains and laughter,
   Retracing
   The unremembered movements
   Of our life,
   Retrieving lost directions
   And forgotten goals.

*Meditation Log*                                    *Date*

9. Times that have been lost to us
Return
And become present
As we seek them
In the quiet waters.
Events old and new
Fit together
As we look within,
Finding the path of our life
Finding the path of our life.

10 Eyes closed in stillness
Breathing comes slow
And deep.
Breathing
Inward, outward,
Slowly.
The waters within us
Settle
And become clear,
Reflecting
From the deep places.

*Meditation Log*                                    *Date*

11. Images taking shape
In the stillness of the water,
Forming,
Changing,
Re-forming,
Reflections of our life,
Events old and new
Revealed in them.
Imagery of our life,
Events old and new
And things still to come,
Reflecting the path of our life,
Reflecting the path of our life
In the Silence . . . In the Silence.

# III

## The Center Point
## Within Me

*Meditation Log*                                        *Date*

1. We are resting,
   Physically quiet,
   Breath and body
   In gentle harmony
   Holding the stillness within.

2. Holding the stillness within,
   Thoughts fit into place.
   No longer spinning,
   They come together;
   No longer disputing,
   Our thoughts
   Are friendly with each other.
   The quality of wholeness
   Replaces
   The discord of the mind.

*Meditation Log*                    *Date*

3.  Mind and body
    Together,
    Thoughts and emotions
    Revolving around
    A single center point.
    Varied movements
    Actively churning
    Form a quiet center.
    A quiet center forms
    In their midst.

4.  We feel the center of our Self,
    The inner center of our Self,
    It is neither body
    Nor mind
    But a center point.
    Not this, not that,
    A single center point,
    The inner center of the Self.

*Meditation Log*                                    *Date*

5. In the midst of activity
   Soft, slow breathing
   Sets a balance.
   An inward stillness
   Becomes present.
   The center point within me
   Establishes itself.

6. For each of us it is so.
   A center point within
   Forms itself.
   A center point is present
   Not in space
   But in our being.

7. A center point within me.
   My whole attention
   At that center point,
   Present there in the stillness,
   In the stillness of the Self.

*Meditation Log*                    *Date*

8. Through this center point
   We move inward,
   Inward and downward
   Through a single straight shaft.
   It is as though we go
   Deep into the earth,
   But within our Self.
   Through the center point within
   We go inward,
   Deeper,
   Deeper inward.

9. My life
   Is like the shaft of a well.
   I go deep into it.
   The life of each of us
   Is a well.
   Its sources are deep,
   But it gives water on the surface.
   Now we go inward,
   Moving through our center point,
   Through our center point,
   Deeply inward to explore
   The infinities of our well.

*Meditation Log*        *Date*

10.  Long enough
     We have been on the surface
     Of our life.
     Now we go inward,
     Moving through our center point
     Inward,
     Into the well of our Self,
     Deeply,
     Further inward
     Into the well of our Self.

11.  We move away
     From the surface of things;
     We leave
     The circles of our thoughts,
     Our habits, customs.
     All the shoulds
     And the oughts
     Of our life
     We leave behind.

*Meditation Log*                                    *Date*

12. We leave them on the surface
    While we go inward,
    Into the depth of our life
    Moving through the center point
    Into the well of our Self
    As deeply
    As fully
    As freely as we can.
    Through the center point
    Exploring the deep places.
    Exploring the deep places
    In the Silence . . . In the Silence.

# IV

## *Into the Well of the Self*

*Meditation Log*                    *Date*

1.  Eyes closed
    We move inward
    Through our center point,
    Deeper,
    Further inward
    Into the well of the Self,
    Exploring
    In the silence there,
    In the darkness there.

2.  We move in the darkness
    Trying to see.
    The silent darkness
    Is like muddy water
    Within our Self
    Until it settles,
    Until it clears.
    Then the darkness becomes light.
    It shines.
    The light shines in the darkness,
    In the darkness
    Of the Self

*Meditation Log*                    *Date*

3. Waiting with eyes closed,
   Now we are able to see.
   Here in the midst of the darkness,
   The silence resonates
   And begins to speak to us.
   Here in the darkness,
   Here in the silence
   Of the well of our life,
   We begin to see
   And we begin to hear.

4. We move about
   Exploring,
   Observing,
   And recording
   All that we discover
   In the depths
   Of the well of our life.
   We each go down our own well,
   The well of our life.
   We do not go down another's well
   But only our own,
   Sometimes sending images
   From the deep places
   As messages
   To those around us.

*Meditation Log* *Date*

5.   We move about with freedom
     In the depths
     Of the well of our life.
     We explore privately
     And yet together,
     Exploring the fullness of our life,
     Its joys and sadness,
     Letting our life
     Reflect itself to us
     In forms old and new.

6.   Exploring the deep places
     Our life returns to us.
     Outward experiences
     And inward experiences,
     We taste them again
     And know them as they are
     Without judging them,
     Without being angry or resentful,
     Without being proud,
     Without being ashamed,
     But knowing
     The experiences of our life
     As they have been
     And as they are.

*Meditation Log*                    *Date*

7. Eyes closed
   We are moving inward
   Into the well of our life,
   Into the well of our Self,
   Taking note of what we see
   And what we hear,
   Of what we smell
   And taste and feel,
   Exploring the depth of our life.

8. Exploring the depth of our life,
   Observing and recording,
   We recognize
   The many dimensions
   Of the outer/inner universe
   As they are reflected in us,
   In the silent darkness,
   In the well of our Self.

*Meditation Log*                    *Date*

9.    Reflections of our life,
      Reflections of our Self,
      Personal
      And more than personal,
      Present themselves to us
      Whether we see or hear them.
      These reflections are the *images*
      That reveal to us
      The inner quality of our being,
      The inner quality of our life.


10.   We direct our attention now
      To beholding them.
      We behold them inwardly
      With every sensitivity we possess,
      With every form of sensing,
      Of seeing, hearing,
      Smelling, touching, feeling,
      And especially
      Directly knowing.
      Directly knowing
      We behold inwardly.

*Meditation Log*                    *Date*

11. Every mode of awareness
    Inwardly alert,
    Inwardly perceptive,
    Beholding everywhere
    And everything
    As we move about
    In the well of our Self,
    Exploring,
    Observing,
    Recording,
    In the Silence . . . In the Silence.

# V

## The Downward/Upward
## Journey

*Meditation Log*                                        *Date*

1. We continue.
   We have moved away from the surface.
   We have gone into our life
   To discover and explore
   The depth of our well.

2. In the quiet
   Focusing inward,
   Our breath moves slowly,
   Deeply,
   Inward, outward.
   The breath moves at the center,
   At the center point within;
   The breath moves at the center,
   At the center of the Self.

3. We direct our minds
   To this center piont
   At the inward depth
   Of our Self.
   Our attention is focused there,
   We are present there
   Within our Self.

*Meditation Log*                                    *Date*

4. The center point relaxes.
   It loosens,
   Stretches, opens.
   The center point
   Becomes the shaft of the well
   Within our Self.
   It is opening wider;
   Its walls are softening,
   The shaft within us is opening,
   Making space so we can move
   Further down the well
   Into the depth of our Self.


5. We go inward,
   Inward.
   We go deeper,
   Deeper.
   We go further away
   And ever closer to our Self.
   We move more easily now.
   Being less fearful
   Of what is strange to us,
   We move more naturally,
   Letting ourselves be drawn
   Deeper inward.

*Meditation Log*          *Date*

6. As we move further
   Into the darkness,
   Into the silence,
   We find that the light is ample,
   More than ample.
   Much is shown to us
   In varied phases.

7. Many shapes and forms,
   Sounds and smells,
   Many visions and symbols
   Present themselves
   To the inward eye.
   It is an inward knowing,
   A direct knowing.
   A beholding
   Through our life
   Of dimensions beyond our life.

*Meditation Log*  *Date*

8.    Much that we never perceived before
Is presenting itself to us now.
As these perceptions come to us,
We record them.
We write them as we perceive them.
We go inward to behold them
And we come upward
Briefly, quickly
To record what has been shown to us
At the depth of the well.

9.    We record
So that we shall remember
The atmosphere
And the reality we have known.
In time to come
We shall consider
And reconsider
The multiple messages
That were given to us
At the depth of the well.

## Meditation Log                    Date

10. We go downward
    Slowly and deeply.
    We come upward
    Quickly and briefly
    To write what needs to be recorded,
    Then to return
    To the depth of the well.

11. Again and again
    We complete the cycle
    Of our downward/upward journey.
    Each time
    A little further downward
    And then up;
    Each time
    A little further inward
    And then out;
    Each time a little further
    From the surface of our life
    Moving toward the depth
    Of the well,
    Moving toward the source
    Beyond the well
    A little at a time.

*Meditation Log*                    *Date*

12. We continue
    Our downward/upward journey,
    Our inward/outward journey.
    Beholding inwardly
    We recognize in the darkness
    What cannot be seen
    In the light,
    Recognizing,
    Recording,
    Exploring the deep places
    On our downward/upward journey
    In the Silence ... In the Silence

# VI

## The Waters
## Beyond the Well

*Meditation Log*                              *Date*

1.   We have been going downward
    And then upward,
    Inward and then outward.
    Each time as we go deeper
    The atmosphere softens to us.
    It becomes more comfortable,
    More congenial.
    It absorbs us more warmly.
    We know
    We belong here.

2.   The deeper we go,
    The further
    We move from our daily life,
    The further
    From our accustomed ways.
    We see strange things
    But they are not strange to us.

*Meditation Log*       *Date*

3.    Something in our Self
       Recognizes
       These new perceptions.
       The further downward we go,
       The further inward we go,
       The more we recognize
       That we are coming home,
       Coming home to our Self.

4.    It is good being home,
       Being at home in our Self.
       We can do many things
       Being at home in our Self.
       Moving inward and outward,
       Feeling stronger now
       Than when we began.

*Meditation Log*                                    *Date*

5.    We move inward again
Deeper than before.
We perceive something beyond us,
Beyond the furthest depth
Of our well.
It seems to be the source
Of our well.
It is drawing us toward it,
Drawing us into it.
We willingly go,
Letting ourselves be drawn there.

6.    We go downward and inward
Freely
Letting ourselves be drawn
Through the silent darkness.
We have passed through
The full depth of the well.
Beyond the well
There is a stream.
At last we have come
To the underground stream.

*Meditation Log*                              *Date*

7. All at once
   We are within the underground stream.
   We did not need to enter it.
   It drew us to it.
   It drew us into it.
   We are moving freely
   Within it now.


8. We are exploring
   In the underground stream.
   Its waters are pleasant.
   They flow gently around us
   And they are buoyant.
   They sustain us.
   They support and carry us.
   The stream is deep
   But its waters are buoyant.
   So none can be lost
   In the underground stream.

*Meditation Log*　　　　　　　　　　　　　　*Date*

9.   We are exploring together
In the underground stream.
Each of us came down our own well
Alone
As a private person,
But we are all meeting here
In the underground stream.

10.   All our separate wells
Lead to this underground stream.
It is the deep resource
For all of us.
All our wells draw from it.
It is our source of supply.
These moving waters
Are home for each of us.

*Meditation Log*            *Date*

11.   There are no separations here.
We intermingle freely.
We find that we *know* things,
We see visions,
We hear sounds,
We have perceptions,
Recognitions,
Intuitions of truths
That were mysterious to us before
But here
In the underground stream
We know them directly.

12.   They come to us as symbols,
But the symbols open to us
Like the bud of a flower
And we look into them
Deeply,
Infinitely inward.
The bud opens level after level.
We look
Into the depth of the flower,
Into the depth of the symbol,
Deep, deep,
As deep as the heart can see.

*Meditation Log*                    *Date*

13.    Everything we behold
We draw into our Self.
As we were drawn into the stream
So we draw it into our Self.
The underground stream
Is one with us,
As we are one
With the underground stream.
It flows around us
And it flows within us.
We share
The unity of Being.
We share
The unity of Being
In the Silence ... In the Silence.

# VII

*Sharing The*
*Underground Stream*

*Meditation Log*                              *Date*

1. We have made the journey
   Into the well of our Self
   And beyond our Self
   Into the moving waters
   Of the underground stream.
   Downward/upward,
   Inward again,
   We are here
   In the waters beyond the well.

2. Many awarenesses
   Have been given to us
   In the waters beyond the well.
   Symbols have opened to us,
   Riddles of life,
   Visions of things to come;
   The struggles and harmonies
   In the movement of the universe
   Have disclosed themselves to us
   One by one.

*Meditation Log*                              *Date*

3. Here in the underground stream
   We realize
   That many others
   In earlier times
   Have entered their wells
   And have gone inward
   Until they reached
   The waters beyond the well
   Where we are now.

4. In ancient days
   Jacob went down his well,
   And where he returned
   He placed a stone
   For remembrance.
   In his way, Moses went down,
   And Isaiah and Ezekiel,
   Lao Tse and Zoroaster,
   Gotama Siddhartha,
   Jesus of Nazareth,
   Teresa and Juliana,
   Meister Eckhart,
   George Fox,
   Waldo Emerson and Walt Whitman,
   And many others
   Have gone down their well
   To the underground stream.

*Meditation Log*                    *Date*

5.  These and many more have been here,
    Some famous in history,
    Others unknown,
    But each by direct beholding
    Discovered
    Many marvelous things
    That were shown to them
    Or that they recognized
    And drew to themselves
    In the underground stream.

6.  Those who have gone down their well
    Into the underground stream
    Have done many things
    Upon returning
    To the surface of their lives.
    Some have written books,
    Some have painted and sculpted,
    Some have made philosophies,
    Some have stated doctrines,
    Some have lived their lives
    More fully
    With inward abundance
    And with gentler wisdom
    Than was possible before.

*Meditation Log*                    *Date*

7.    We think of them,
Those who have been here before us,
As we ourselves
Enter the underground stream.
We are not the first
Nor shall we be the last
To go
Through the center point of Self
Into the well
And beyond the well
Into the underground stream.

8.    Now we have entered the stream,
Ourselves
And more than ourselves,
Present to one another
Beyond separateness
In the unity of Being,
Accessible to everyone,
Sharing with all
In the unity of Being.

*Meditation Log*                    *Date*

9.     Sharing the underground stream
We recognize others here,
Not only we who are entering now
But those who have been here before us.
Their quality of being,
Their atmosphere,
Still is present
In the underground stream.

10.    Those who have been here before us
Century upon century
Have left the imprint of their presence
On the waters
Of the underground stream.
Through the quality of their being
They will speak with us.
They will share with us
Their atmosphere
And their awareness,
Their lives and their knowledge,
The quality of their being
In the timeless unity.
In the timeless unity
They will share with us
As one.

*Meditation Log*                    *Date*

11.   Sharing the underground stream
      We are invited to speak,
      To ask our questions,
      To consider the answers
      And to record what is said.
      We are invited to speak,
      To share in dialogue
      Here in the underground stream,
      Listening and speaking
      With those who have entered before us
      And have left their mark
      Upon the atmosphere
      Of the underground stream.
      Their quality of being
      Is awaiting us
      In the timeless waters.

*Meditation Log*                    *Date*

12. Gratefully
    We greet them,
    Speaking and listening,
    Our hearts open to their wisdom,
    Asking and hearing,
    Speaking of all life,
    Speaking of our life,
    With those who have been here before us.
    Their quality of being is present,
    Present for us now.
    We are speaking and listening
    In the Silence . . . In the Silence.

# VIII

*Entering the*
*Cathedral*

*Meditation Log*                              *Date*

1.  Much we have learned
    In the underground stream,
    Some that was shown to us,
    Some that was spoken to us.
    We draw it all into our Self
    As we were drawn
    Into the underground stream.
    We shall continue to absorb it
    And learn from it
    Now that we know how to reach
    And enter
    The underground stream.

2.  Those who have been there before us
    Have much to teach us
    Of what they learned there
    And what took place
    When they returned
    From the underground stream.

*Meditation Log*                                    *Date*

3.  Where they came back,
    Where they emerged from the well,
    Many placed a stone for remembrance
    As Jacob had done.
    And many others,
    Who did not themselves
    Reach the depth of the stream,
    Also placed a stone
    To commemorate
    The remarkable event
    Of which they had heard.

4.  Each placed a stone
    As a token
    And many placed their stones
    Together,
    One building upon the other,
    Until soon
    A magnificent cathedral
    Covered the well,
    The well that led
    To the underground stream.

*Meditation Log*         *Date*

5. Since that time
   Many have come to the cathedral
   To pay their respects,
   To praise the name of their God,
   To ask favors of many kinds.
   They all seem to know
   That something important is there,
   That something important is present
   At the site of the cathedral.

6. The well
   That leads to the underground stream
   Is at the base of the cathedral.
   But now it is covered by stones
   And difficult to fine.

7. How shall we get to the well
   Now that it has been covered
   By the stones of the cathedral,
   Now that it has been hidden
   By the passage
   Of the centuries?

*Meditation Log*                    *Date*

8. We have found a way.
   We can go there together.
   There is a shaft of a well
   Beneath the cathedral.
   And where is the cathedral?
   We have nowhere to look
   And nowhere to go,
   For you are the cathedral,
   I am the cathedral.
   The way to the underground stream
   Is the well
   That is hidden within us.


9. Wherever we are
   Our cathedral is present;
   When we seek a quiet place
   In the midst of turmoil,
   A refuge
   From the pressures of the world,
   Wherever we are,
   Whatever is happening
   Our cathedral is present
   And open for us.

*Meditation Log*             *Date*

10. Entering the cathedral
    Is sanctuary
    From the hurricanes of life,
    A quiet center
    Wherever we are,
    Whatever is happening.

11. Entering the cathedral
    We become still;
    Our eyes closed,
    We breathe slowly,
    Inward, outward,
    Feeling the center of our body,
    Feeling the center of our Self,
    Feeling the center point within.

*Meditation Log*          *Date*

12. Entering the cathedral
    We focus inward,
    Directing ourselves
    Through the center point within.
    The muddy waters of our life
    Become tranquil and clear,
    They become a mirror
    Reflecting within us
    The depths and heights of being.
    Thus the way inward
    Opens to us.
    We find the well
    Beneath the cathedral.

*Meditation Log*                                    *Date*

13. Entering the cathedral
    Wherever we may be,
    The center point within us
    Becomes the well
    That opens inward.
    We move into that well
    And beyond it
    Into the buoyant waters
    Of the underground stream
    Where we are now . . .
    Joining those
    Who have been here before us
    In the timeless unity,
    In the timeless unity
    Where we are now
    In the Silence . . . In the Silence.

# *Part Three*

# PERSPECTIVES

# 1. From the Anonymous Monk to the Modern Person

We have seen that our work with *The Well and the Cathedral* proceeds step by step, level by level, cycle by cycle. As one unit of meditation is completed, another is set into motion. Each feeds into and becomes the starting point for the next, so that our spiritual work builds a chain of experiences reaching depths, touching peaks, progressively expanding the range of our awareness and refining the quality of our being.

When we consider the continuity of our experience over a period of time, we realize that our inner quest proceeds as though it has a life of its own. It is drawn forward by a guidance that unfolds from within us, moving in directions and making discoveries that could not have been anticipated when the work began. Without understanding the reasons, we find ourselves being led to our next steps, often in the midst of confusion and disappointment, and sometimes despair. Even those beliefs and actions that might be regarded as errors eventually become teachers to us as we continue on our quest.

In a profound sense there is no such thing as making mistakes on the spiritual dimension of life. All our experiences feed into a single inner process that self-adjusts as it proceeds. At each point it establishes a new balance in which the contents of our life are each given a place and a value that is appropriate to that moment. As we add new experiences, whether they satisfy or disturb us, they bring about a readjustment to a new condition of balance, and thus take us an additional step along our way.

Each of us, a unique individual in the universe, is striving to connect with a truth that is valid for everyone. We are reaching toward universals of meaning, but since we can see our truths only through the coloration of our life experience, we call them by many different names. What is more important, it is a truth that presents itself in many degrees. We may have some degree of it but not all of it, just as we may eat some of the fruit on a tree but not all.

There are many models in history of persons who built their lives spiritually by degrees, proceeding a step at a time. One of these was the fourteenth century monk who wrote *The Cloud of Unknowing*. While preparing this edition of *The Well and the Cathedral* I have found myself thinking back to 1956 when I transposed that text into modern English, mainly to help myself follow the subtleties of the anonymous monk so that I could undertake his meditations.

At that time I recommended the monk's approach partly because of his earthy, realistic, humorous, no-nonsense style of dealing with the delicate phenomena of the inner life; partly because of the breadth of perspective that enabled him to see beyond the boundaries of the medieval world to the universals of spirit; and especially because of the experimental attitude he brought to the entire realm of spiritual involvement. As a spiritual pragmatist, the monk of *The Cloud of Unknowing* followed the same trial-and-error approach that a modern empiricist uses in a laboratory. But he applied it to the life of the spirit.

The goal of the monk was to experience connection with the great Unity of Being, which he called God and referred to in the medieval language of churchly observance. But he approached his goal in a way that has much in common with the spirit of modern science. Nonetheless, when I called the monk's work to the attention of the public at that time there was very little response. In those days there were relatively few in western civilization who acknowledged the value of working actively in the processes of the inner life. The prevailing tone of the culture was extroverted and rationalistic, and people appreciated the importance only of hard tangible facts. To speak of being empirical and experimental with respect to the elusive intangibles of the inner life seemed to be a contradiction in terms.

Attitudes have changed since then, however, and the last decade especially has brought a greater appreciation of the vision of the anonymous monk as well as similar historical efforts. Nowadays when I speak of his experimental approach to spiritual experience, it receives a much friendlier response.

However, there is a major difficulty that still prevents the modern person from becoming involved in the monk's program: the medieval Christian symbolism which the monk used as the vehicle for his profound spiritual contact is now for cultural reasons an obstacle to many persons. Rather than serving as a vehicle for them, it is a barrier between their inner selves and the unitary connective experience. And yet, as my contact with large numbers of persons has increased during the past years, it has become clear to me that many are seeking essentially the same experience of unity that the monk was describing. But to the twentieth century ear, the monk's cultural tone and the historical symbols in which he expressed his experiences have an alien sound. Because the language belongs to an earlier, now foreign, and largely rejected time of history, the words can be heard but not the meaning behind them.

This barrier to the message of the monk of *The Cloud of Unknowing* also prevents many persons from recognizing the validity of other paths to spiritual connection described by historical figures who reached the unitary experience. When the spiritual teachers of earlier times set out to convey the particular truth they had found, or to teach the steps by which they came to it, they could do so only in terms of the symbols and images that had been the carriers of their experience. And yet the life of each had a specific dateline in history. Each came from a particular culture that left its characteristic imprint upon it. And each bore the marks of the subjective depths, the private encounter with the ultimates of existence, that distinguished their unique experience. These particularities are their trademark, like the monk's medieval symbolism in *The Cloud of Unknowing*. Sometimes the symbols open a road that enables others to share the experience of spiritual teachers in history. But very often the symbols become barriers that separate us from the original unitary contact that they brought about.

In the course of my own searchings, I have had the occasion to know both of these experiences. Sometimes I have been able to share the inner contact of the great teachers by entering the symbols that were their vehicles. At other times their symbols have become barriers to me because I was unable to penetrate their exterior.

Eventually I learned that whenever I was able to move inward deeply enough, I could participate to some degree in the connective experience they had achieved. At those times it was as though I swam underwater beneath the blockages presented by their particular symbols and doctrines so that I was able to reach the core of their experience. Thus their inner wisdom became accessible without the impediments of their outer trappings.

This way of interior connection has helped me penetrate the surface of the teachings and disciplines that I have explored over the years: zen, contemplative Christianity, Hasidism, various cosmic philosophers and poets, Lao Tse, Sufism, and especially the prophetic spirit of the Old Testament. The influence of each of these teachings as well as of others, is to be found in the text of *The Well and the Cathedral*, although the symbolism of none is expressed directly.

Something more important, however, than their symbolism is very strongly present. It is the underlying process by which each achieved a unitary connection that gave an energy and a meaning to their lives. As we work toward this in our modern situation, the question of what such a unitary connection involves becomes of great significance, especially in relation to our experience with *The Wall and the Cathedral*.

In the introductory sentence he placed at the head of his book, the monk says, "This is a book of contemplation called *The Cloud of Unknowing* in which a soul is united with God." In the original version, the medieval phrase he used was "oned with God" and the additional overtones there clarify the experience. "Unitary connection" means to be united in the sense of "being made one with" a reality that is other than and larger than oneself. But in the moment when we become one with it, it no longer is an "other" to us, and we are no longer an "other" to it. We have become united with it, connected in such a way that there is no separation between us.

This unity of being is sometimes spoken of as love. It is not love in the sense of a feeling of affection, but love in the profound Biblical sense of "knowing" in both actual and symbolic terms. As when Adam "knew" Eve, it was an act of oneness in which opposites were connected in unity.

The experience of oneness encompasses and overcomes the separateness of human existence. It transcends the conflicts and competitiveness of society, and to that degree it opens a way to human transformation. But what does the experience of unity actually involve?

Individuals perceive and describe it variously. For some it is a union with the universe, a melting away of the person in a suffusion of cosmic wholeness. This is what Freud referred to as the "oceanic feeling." He said he respected those who reported having had such experiences, but that he was temperamentally unable to understand what they were describing.

For others, Unity of Being is a more specific

connective experience, as when the monk speaks of seeking oneness between God and the soul. We have to interpret that in terms of the symbolic framework of his mind and the context of his culture. To the monk, God is the one reality that has meaning in the universe. Indeed, to the monk God *is* meaning; and everything else is relative to that reality.

When the monk speaks of the "soul," it has more than one aspect. On one level, he means by the soul the specific individual entity that is the object of salvation within the worldview of Christianity. The full spiritual discipline he sets forth in his treatise, however, indicates that his understanding of the "soul" has an additional and more encompassing scope. To him the soul is the whole interior realm within which the struggles and the strivings of the spirit are experienced. It is the space within us where the work of reaching toward unity with God is to be carried through. It contains the resources, the energies, the qualities, and the "stirrings," like the "image of God" within, that supply us and enable us to pursue the goal of unity.

The monk's larger understanding of the soul gives us a clue as to how the experience of unitary connection can be approached in the modern world. His narrower, more specific view of the soul is limited to those who share in his traditional concept and hold it as an article of faith. On the other hand, his larger view of the soul, as the universe within ourselves where spiritual work is carried through, provides a perspective in which all of us can seek the unitary experience. The first concept is one that is bound by a particular culture and tradition. While it does afford an experience of connection, it can do so only within its own terms. But the larger view of the soul gives us a range that reaches beyond special beliefs. It gives us a perspective in which the experience of unitary connection between the outer cosmic universe and the inner universe of the self can be appreciated without being limited by particular cultural/historical symbols or beliefs.

Over the years these reflections on the anonymous monk of *The Cloud of Unknowing* have sharpened for me the distinction between the outer forms in which spiritual experiences take place and the inner process by means of which they unfold. Interestingly enough, it is the outer forms of traditional faith that are breaking down in modern times and that breakdown has highly significant effects. It throws people back upon themselves and forces them to pay attention to the validity of the experiences that occur within the depth of their own inner universe.

For many of us, to be thrown back upon ourselves becomes a frightening, almost nightmarish experience. We feel there are no resources for us to draw upon and we fall into the anxiety state which the existentialist phraseology describes as the "dread" at finding "no exit" from the dilemmas of existence. Psychiatry, looking at the same situation, sees it meriting a diagnosis of neurosis. But our experience with *The Well and the Cathedral* opens another possibility. It takes us on a narrow pathway inward that eludes existential dread on the one side and medical diagnosis on the other while it carries us to the depths of our being.

# 2. The Unitary Connection

When the historical traditions lose their power to guide us, we are turned back to the resources of our own individuality. There we experience our all-too-human limitations and the feelings of anxiety that are inherent in being a finite person in an infinite universe. As we proceed into the depths of the Self, however, we come to a place that is beyond dread and diagnosis, beyond both the darkness of existentialism and the pathology of medicine. It is an inward place, and we reach it when we have gone far enough into the well of our Self to enter the underground stream.

Numerous new awarenesses come to us here and they have a renewing effect. Many of the conditions that psychiatry has interpreted as illnesses are healed here. The reason for this is primarily that contact with the underground stream gives a light of meaning for the existential darkness. We realize, then, that as we move inward through the well of Self, we are taking steps toward wholeness as we are deepening the relationship between our individuality and the universe.

The underground stream is a place of unity where experiences of personal and cosmic wholeness are brought about. Considered as a symbol or as a teaching, the underground stream is altogether neutral and altogether accepting. It rejects none but it has room for every type of doctrine. In the underground stream beliefs that seem to be in opposition can come together and draw each other toward wholeness. At that deep level the fluid sense of time makes room for change and incorporates it into the process of spiritual growth. Differences in philosophy that sometimes seem to be in sharp contradiction to one another are absorbed into the continuation of history. By means of their conflict, the unitary connections of life are being reinforced and made more profound.

When we speak of the underground stream, we recognize it to be the same as the place to which the monk of *The Cloud of Unknowing* was referring when he spoke of "The ground of naked being." It is the place where "oneness with God" may be known as a reality and where we can experience unitary connection with life. Since it is a place that can be described by many different names, it is beyond the phraseology of any particular religion. Yet it enables us to recognize the core of truth in many religions.

A primary contribution of the anonymous monk lies in the concept and method he provided for working toward unitary experience. His limitation and his unavailability for the modern mind comes from the fact that the symbolic forms in which he presented his program necessarily reflected the attitudes and beliefs of his time. Modern persons who are not in tune with those medieval constructs necessarily find it difficult to follow the monk's instructions even though they are intuitively in accord with his goals. There is, however, a way of interior practice that corresponds to the process the monk recommended for achieving a unifying contact with the ground of Being. Using a neutral set of symbols as their vehicle, the sequence of meditations with which we have just worked in *The Well and the Cathedral* serve as a modern equivalent to the procedures of *The Cloud of Unknowing*.

The essence of his format and method is contained in his view of the soul as a large interior area in which the practical work of unitary experience can be carried through. Step by step he moves into the depths of the inner space of the soul until the atmosphere in which he finds himself is markedly different from his accustomed condition of rational consciousness. It is a "Cloud of Unknowing" which not only is placed between him and his God but also serves as the deep ground of meeting where the unitary connection can be established as an abiding quality of his personal being.

The monk's ultimate goal is to achieve unity with God. Toward this, he describes as his core spiritual process a series of interior cycles through which one must pass again and again. The eight units of experience in *The Well and the Cathedral* traverse an inward path that parallels this as it follows its principle of progressive deepening through a full cycle of meditation. It does this, however, in a context of symbolism that is more accessible to the modern mind not only because it is neutral with respect to religious doctrine, but because of its universality in the larger perspective of history. The symbol of the well, for example, has appeared in spiritual writings since the most ancient days as a representation of the path of spiritual connection. So pervasive has its use in this way been over the centuries that the symbolic associations it evokes are now virtually self evident. As a modern metaphor it enables us to move toward unitary contact in neutral terms that fulfill a religious function while they are also in accord with our psychological understanding.

The symbol of the well implies individuality, insofar as each well is separate from every other well, just as each life is separate from every other life. As we descend into the well of Self, therefore, we move through levels of experience that reflect our personal existence. Personal memory is the first of these. We recall the events of our life.

"Exploring the deep places,
Our life returns to us."

Moving deeper, we come to a level of memory that is much more than personal. It is the memory of history, of experiences that belong not to ourselves alone but to the memory of humankind. Awarenessescome to us that are derived from events we have not experienced personally, but which in some mysterious way have left their traces in our consciousness.

> "Personal memories,
> And mysteries
> Much more than personal."

We find ourselves being brought into touch with circumstances and beliefs that express the encounter with reality not of ourselves but of the lives of other persons in other times and places. As we move further into the depths of our well, we are given glimpses of events that pertain to others in our genealogy, in our historical line of inheritance, and others in our cultural or religious tradition. Sometimes we are given awareness of events that are far removed from our particular path in history, drawn from cultures and traditions that are foreign to us. They may seem to be foreign, but they are not alien to us. When we are given glimpses of them as we move through our well, an understanding of the larger dimensions of their meaning also comes to us.

We find that we have cognitions of symbolic and other mysteries of life greater than any knowledge we had learned or been taught on the outer level of our experience. As we move down into our well, we find that we are able to know things that we did not think we knew. Knowledge comes to us beyond our individual experiences. History speaks to us on many levels, depending on the sensitivity to it that our practice has given us. We gain a greater understanding of events that relate to our individual life, and also an intuitive awareness of the universals of human experience. The deeper we go into our well, the further we move beyond the subjectivities of our individual life and the more directly we touch fundamental truths of existence.

The metaphor of the well represents the individuality and uniqueness of our life, but the further we go into it the more completely we transcend the separateness of our ego-existence. It expresses the profound paradox that the more we move inward into our privacy and individuality, the more we become connected to the wholeness and richness of the universe. At its deeper levels we experience an expansion of consciousness that enables us to feel we are not limited to being only ourselves. We move through the well of the Self into a dimension beyond it, and that is when we come to the underground stream. Here we experience the Unity of Being and are one with it. It is the place of transcendence where, after a long inward journey, self-transformation and renewal begin.